Ella May's
FAVORITE
RECIPES

Compiled by

Ella May Miller

Heart to Heart Speaker

HEART TO HEART®

HARRISONBURG, VIRGINIA

Introduction

"Take cooking out of the home" is the slogan of a famous restaurant in one large city.

I, for one, do not share this sentiment! Nourishing and tempting meals at home is the right of every husband and child.

Another philosophy of mine is that simple foods are the healthful foods. The Bible story of Daniel and his friends, who chose to eat vegetables and common foods rather than the rich food from the King's table, has indelibly engraved this truth on my mind. However, on special occasions and when entertaining I turn to these recipes for something different.

These recipes come from many homes, across the country and abroad. If you should find one of yours in these pages accept that as the family's sincere appreciation of the recipe. It is with great pleasure that I pass these on to you.

Ella May Miller

Table of Contents

3 Beverages
4 Breads
8 Cakes
13 Candy
17 Cereals
18 Cookies
23 Desserts
28 Eggs and Cheese Dishes
31 Fish
32 Jams and Jellies
34 Meats
40 Pickles and Relishes
42 Pies
46 Salads
49 Soups
52 Vegetables
56 Holiday Traditions
60 Miscellaneous
62 Hints

Beverages

I enjoy hot drinks--the year around. But cool, refreshing ones are not to be ignored.

EGGNOG

4 eggs	1/8 t. nutmeg
4 c. milk (cold)	1/8 t. salt
½ t. vanilla	1/3 c. sugar

Beat eggs thoroughly. Add remaining ingredients. Beat with a rotary beater until frothy.

GRAPE JUICE

1 c. Concord grapes	Boiling water
½ c. sugar	

Wash grapes and put them in a sterile quart jar. Add sugar. Slowly fill jar with boiling water. Stir to dissolve sugar. Seal. Let ripen at least 4 weeks before serving.

MILK COFFEE

1/3 c. strong coffee infusion (use double amount of coffee, either percolated or instant). Fill cup with hot milk. Add sugar to taste.

Tea (double strength) may be substituted for coffee. This makes a tasty hot breakfast drink, or at "coffee break."

MINT TEA

Fresh garden tea	2 lemons
2 qt. boiling water	2/3 c. sugar

Wash tea. Place in large pan or mixing bowl (not aluminum). Pour boiling water over tea. Steep 10-15 min. Fill large pitcher 1/2 full with ice cubes. Add sugar and thinly sliced lemons. Pour tea (strained) over ice. Stir until sugar is dissolved. ·If necessary add more ice. Serve immediately. A most refreshing summer drink!

Variations: Use desired quantity of tea and water. Steep, (or boil 5 min.) and serve hot with sugar and lemon, or with milk.

Breads

Ever since a dear neighbor lady, 11 years ago, started treating my boys to slices of fresh bread dripping with butter and honey, I've had to bake. We do enjoy the homemade bread, as well as the quick breads. Come Saturday it's time for cinnamon rolls.

BREAD

6 c. hot water
1 pkg. dry yeast
4 tb. sugar

4 tb. shortening
2 tb. salt
16 c. pre-sifted flour

Add shortening, sugar and salt to water. When lukewarm, add yeast. When dissolved, add flour. Knead dough until smooth and elastic. Place in greased pan. Cover and set in warm place to rise until double in bulk. Shape into loaves. Place in well-greased bread pans. Brush with shortening and allow to rise again until double in size. Bake at 425° for 15 min. Reduce to 350° for 35 min. When baked remove from pan. If you desire crusty bread do not cover while cooling. Makes 4 large or 5 medium loaves.

<u>Buns</u>: When ready to shape into loaves, take out desired amount of dough and shape into small buns. Place in greased pan. Brush with butter. When double in size bake at 400° for 20-25 minutes. Serve warm.

BISCUITS

2 c. flour
4 t. baking powder
½ t. salt

3 tb. shortening
1 c. milk

Sift dry ingredients. Work in shortening until like coarse corn meal. Add liquid all at once. Stir. Drop from large spoon onto greased cookie sheet.
NOTE: Use sour milk, 3 t. baking powder and 1/2 t. soda.

Substitute wheat or graham flour for one-half of white flour.

FOUNDATION SWEET DOUGH

1 c. scalded milk	1½ t. salt
1 c. lukewarm water	2 eggs, beaten
1 cake yeast	7 c. flour
¼ c. margarine	½ c. sugar

Scald milk and pour over sugar, salt and shortening. Dissolve yeast in lukewarm water. When milk has cooled to lukewarm temperature, add yeast and beaten eggs. Mix well. Add flour gradually, beating well. Knead lightly, working in just enough flour so that dough can be handled. Place dough in a greased bowl, cover and let stand in a warm place. Let rise until double in bulk (about 2 hrs.).Make into cinnamon or "sticky" rolls.

CINNAMON ROLLS

One recipe of foundation sweet dough.

6 tb. melted butter	1 tb. cinnamon
1½ c. brown sugar	1 c. raisins

Divide raised dough into two portions. Roll into oblong pieces 1/4" thick. Brush with melted butter. Sprinkle with brown sugar, cinnamon and raisins. Roll like a jelly roll. With a sharp knife cut slices 1/2" thick. Place slices 1" apart on greased tin with cut side down. Let rise in warm place until light (about one hour). Bake at 400° for 20-25 minutes.

"STICKY" ROLLS

Make 1 recipe of foundation sweet dough. Roll out as for cinnamon rolls. Sprinkle with cinnamon. Roll out as jelly roll. Slice 1/2" thick. Place slices in a pan with syrup. Let rise until double in size. Bake at 350° for approx. 30 minutes.

Syrup

1 c. brown sugar	1/3 c. cream
½ c. nut meats	2 tb. soft butter

Melt butter, add cream, sugar and nut meats. Stir over low heat until all blended. Pour into pan.

GRIDDLE CAKES

1¼ c. flour	1 egg, well beaten
1 tb. sugar	1 c. milk
2½ t. baking powder	2 tb. shortening
½ t. salt	

Sift dry ingredients. Combine egg, milk, and melted shortening (slightly cooled) and turn into a well made in dry ingredients. Combine liquid and dry ingredients gradually. Mix thoroughly until smooth. Bake on hot griddle.

NOTE: Substitute sour for sweet milk and use 1/2 t. soda and 1/2 t. baking powder.

Substitute 1/2 c. or less of whole wheat for equal amount of flour. Add more liquid.

CORN BREAD

1 1/3 c. white flour	5 t. baking powder
2/3 c. corn meal	½ t. salt
1–2 tb. sugar	1 egg (beaten)
2–4 tb. shortening	1 c. milk

(If sour milk is used, change leavening to ½ t. soda and 3 t. baking powder.)

Sift dry ingredients together into mixing bowl. Add egg, milk and shortening, and stir just enough to mix ingredients. Pour in greased shallow pan. Bake 30 min. at 350°.

FRIED CORN MEAL MUSH

3 c. yellow corn meal	1 t. salt
2 qts. boiling water	½ c. white flour

Bring 1 1/2 qt. water to a boil in heavy aluminum or iron kettle. Thoroughly mix corn meal, flour and salt. Add the remaining 1/2 qt. water to form a paste. Slowly add the paste to boiling water. Stir constantly. Cover and cook over low heat approx. one hour. Stir occasionally. Pour mush into flat pans, or bread pans, to mold. When cold, slice 1/4" thick and fry until golden brown. Serve with syrup or apple butter, or meat gravy or "pudding."

NOTE: Before pouring mush into pans, serve with milk and sugar (or salt).

GERMAN SOUR CREAM TWISTS

3½ c. sifted flour
1 t. salt
1 c. shortening (part butter)
1 pkg. dry yeast
¼ c. warm water

¾ c. thick sour cream (20%)
1 whole egg and 2 egg yolks,
    well beaten
1 t. vanilla
1 c. sugar

Sift flour, salt into mixing bowl. Cut in shortening. Dissolve
yeast in water. Stir in flour mixture with sour cream, eggs,
vanilla. Mix well with hand. Cover with damp cloth and re-
frigerate 2 hrs. Roll half of dough on sugared board into an
oblong 8x16". Fold ends toward center, ends overlapping.
Sprinkle with sugar, roll again to same size. Repeat a third
time. Roll about 1/4" thick. Cut into strips 1x4". Twist
ends in opposite directions--stretching dough slightly. Put
in shape of horseshoe on ungreased baking sheet--pressing
ends to keep shape. Repeat with rest of dough. Heat oven to
375° (quick moderate). Bake about 15 min. or until delicately
browned. Take from baking sheet immediately. Makes about
5 dozen. (Delicious iced with a bit of orange frosting(p. 22).

FRENCH BREAKFAST PUFFS

1/3 c. soft shortening (part butter)
½ c. sugar
1 egg
1½ c. sifted flour

½ t. salt
1½ t. baking powder
¼ t. nugmeg
½ c. milk

Thoroughly mix shortening, sugar and egg. Sift together dry
ingredients. Add to mixture alternately with milk. Fill
greased muffin cups 2/3 full. Bake at 350°, until golden
brown (20-25 min.). Immediately roll in mixture of 1/2 c.
sugar and 1 t. cinnamon. Serve hot.

*"Man shall not live by bread alone, but by every word of
God."* Matt. 4:4

Cakes

I often bake a cake in a large pan and do not remove it--usually
uniced. The pan is emptied soon enough! But when I prefer a
nice cake these recipes supply me with a good choice. Angel
food is for birthdays.

UP-SIDE DOWN CAKE

1½ c. cake or 1¼ c. bread flour	1 egg well beaten
2 t. baking powder	½ c. milk
½ t. salt	1 t. flavoring
½ c. sugar	¼ c. melted shortening

Measure and sift dry ingredients. Combine egg, milk, flavoring, and shortening (slightly cooked). Turn into dry ingredients.
Beat thoroughly. Pour this over fruit-sugar mixture in baking
pan:

Fruit Mixture

4 tb. butter   Peaches or pineapple
1 c. brown sugar

Arrange fruit in bottom of buttered baking pan. Dot with butter.
Evenly sprinkle with sugar. Bake at 375° for about 30 minutes.
Remove to serving dish, turning it upside down. Serve with hard
sauce or whipped cream.

SOUR CREAM CAKE

1 egg, unbeaten	1 ¾ c. cake or 1½ c. bread flour
About 3/4 c. sour cream	1¼ t. baking powder
1 c. sugar	¼ t. soda
1 t. vanilla	¼ t. salt

Drop egg into cup,. fill with cream, turn into a bowl. Add sugar,
slowly beating as it is added. Add vanilla. Add sifted dry ingredients and beat about 2 minutes to combine thoroughly. Pour
into greased or lined pan (8" x 8" x 2 1/2") and bake in moderate
oven, 360° for about 30 minutes.
NOTE: For sweet cream, omit soda and increase baking powder to 2 1/4 t.

ANNIVERSARY CHIFFON CAKE

2¼ c. sifted cake flour
¾ c. sugar
¾ c. brown sugar (packed)
3 t. baking powder
1 t. salt
½ c. vegetable oil
5 eggs yolks, unbeaten

¾ c. cold water
2 t. maple flavoring
½ t. cream of tartar
1 c. egg whites (7-8)
1 c. very finely chopped
   pecans

Heat oven to 325°. Sift dry ingredients into bowl. Make a well; add oil, egg yolks, water, flavoring. Beat with spoon until smooth. Beat egg whites and cream of tartar in large mixing bowl to form very stiff peaks. Pour egg yolk mixture gradually over beaten whites, gently folding with rubber scraper just until blended. Gently fold in pecans. Pour into ungreased tube pan 10"x4". Bake at 325° for 55 min., then at 350° for 10 to 15 min. longer, or until top springs back when lightly touched. Invert on funnel. Let hang until cold. Frost with following cream icing:

Whipped Cream Icing

Put 2 cups whipping cream and 3/4 c. brown sugar (packed) in mixing bowl; chill completely. When cold, whip to desired consistency. Divide cake into 3 layers, putting 1 c. whipped cream mixture between each layer. Frost top and sides of cake with remaining whipped cream mixture. (Cake may be kept whole and iced with whipped cream.)

ANGEL FOOD CAKE

1 c. cake flour
1¼ c. sugar
1½ c. egg whites (11-12 eggs)
2 tb. water

½ t. salt
1 t. cream of tartar
1 t. vanilla

Sift and measure flour. Sift three times with 1/2 c. sugar. Beat egg whites until frothy. Add cream of tartar and salt. Beat until whites hold peaks. With wire whisk slowly fold in remaining sugar. Add flavoring. Sift sugar-flour mixture over egg whites, 2 tablespoons at a time. Fold in lightly. Blend well and pour into an ungreased large tube pan (10"). Cut through batter with a knife. Bake at 350° for 1 hour. Remove from oven and invert pan to cool.

Variation: 1) Substitute 1/2 t. almond extract for 1 t. vanilla.
            2) Remove 3 tb. flour from cup, add 3 tb. cocoa.

GLAZED ORANGE CAKE

1 c. butter or margarine
2 c. sugar
½ t. vanilla
2 tb. grated orange rind
5 eggs
3 c. cake flour

1 tb. baking powder
Pinch of salt
¾ c. milk

Glaze
¼ c. butter or margarine
2/3 c. sugar
1/3 c. orange juice

Butter and flour a 10" tube pan. Cream butter or margarine and sugar until light and fluffy. Add vanilla and orange rind. Add eggs, one at a time, beating well after each addition. Sift together twice the cake flour, baking powder and salt. Add to the creamed mixture a little at a time, alternately with the milk, ending up with flour, beating well after each addition. Spoon into prepared tube pan. Bake in a moderate oven, 350° for about 1 hr. or until top of cake springs back when touched. Cool pan on wire cake rack for 2 minutes.

Heat ingredients for glaze in a saucepan until sugar is dissolved. Pour evenly over cake in pan while cake is still hot. Allow cake to cool thoroughly in tube pan before removing.

ORANGE CHIFFON CAKE

In first bowl, sift together:
   2¼ c. sifted cake flour
   1½ c. sugar

1 t. salt
3 t. baking powder

Make a well and add these:
   ½ c. cooking oil
   5 unbeaten egg yolks

¾ c. cold water
Grated rind of 2 oranges
   (about 3 tbs.)

Beat with spoon until smooth.

In large second bowl put:
   1 c. egg whites (7-8)
   ½ t. cream of tartar

Beat into very stiff peaks, stiffer than for meringue. DO NOT UNDERBEAT.

Pour egg yolk mixture gradually over beaten egg whites, gently folding with rubber scraper just until blended. DON'T STIR. Pour immediately into ungreased 10" tube pan. Bake 55 min. at 325°, then increase to moderate (350°) for 10 to 15 min., or until top springs back when lightly touched. Invert to cool.

TOASTED SPICE CAKE

½ c. shortening
2 c. brown sugar
2 eggs
2½ c. cake flour
½ t. salt
1 t. soda

1 t. baking powder
1½ t. cinnamon
1 t. cloves
1¼ c. sour milk
1 t. vanilla

Cream shortening. Gradually add sugar. Beat until fluffy. Add egg yolks and beat again. Sift flour; measure and add salt, soda, baking powder and spices. Sift again. Add dry ingredients alternately with milk and flavoring. Beat thoroughly after each addition. Pour into a greased flat pan 8 x 12 x 1 1/4 inches. Bake at 350° for 40 min. When baked, spread on the following mixture:

1 c. brown sugar
1 c. coconut

1/3 c. soft butter
¼ c. cream

Toast slightly under broiler.

ECONOMY DEVIL'S FOOD CAKE

2 c. sugar
½ c. butter or lard
2 eggs
½ c. cocoa

1 c. sweet milk
1 t. soda
2 c. flour
2 t. vanilla

Cream shortening and sugar. Add eggs and beat well. Dissolve cocoa in 1/2 c. hot water, beat smooth and add to mixture. Add milk and vanilla. Add soda sifted with flour 3 times, beat well. Pour into greased layer pans. Bake at 350° for 25-30 minutes.

JEANNE'S CAKE

1 c. butter
2 c. sugar
4 eggs
3 c. cake flour

½ t. salt
3 t. baking powder
1 c. sweet cream
1 t. vanilla

Cream shortening. Add sugar gradually and beat until fluffy. Add eggs, 1 at a time and beat until light. Sift flour; measure. Add salt and baking powder. Sift again. Add dry ingredients alternately with cream and flavoring. Beat thoroughly after each addition. Pour into large, greased loaf pan. Bake at 350° for 1 hour.

PINEAPPLE FLUFF CAKE

6 egg whites	1 tb. lemon juice
¼ t. salt	½ c. unsweetened pine-
¾ c. sugar	apple juice
6 egg yolks	1½ c. cake flour
¾ c. sugar	1 t. baking powder

Beat egg whites with salt to form moist, glossy peaks. Gradually beat in 3/4 c. sugar. Beat egg yolks and 3/4 c. sugar until thick; add lemon and pineapple juices; beat until sugar dissolves. Add flour sifted with baking powder. Fold in egg whites. Bake in 10-inch ungreased, angel-cake pan in moderate oven (325°) 1 hour. Invert to cool.

QUICK CARAMEL FROSTING

½ c. butter	1¾ to 2 c. confectioners
1 c. brown sugar	sugar
¼ c. milk	

Melt butter; add brown sugar and cook over low heat two min., stirring constantly. Add milk and continue to stir until mixture comes to a boil. Remove from heat and cool. Add confectioner's sugar until of right consistency to spread.

SEVEN MINUTE FROSTING

	1 tb. honey or corn syrup or
3 tb. water	1/8 t. cream of tartar
1 egg white	1/8 t. salt
1 c. sugar	1 t. flavoring

Place all ingredients except flavoring in upper part of double boiler. Beat the mixture with rotary egg beater, beating rapidly at first, then steadily and continuously for about 7 min. Keep water boiling in lower part of double boiler during the beating. Remove from stove, pour out hot water and fill with cold water, and replace upper part of double boiler. Allow it to stand 5 min. Add flavoring and stir,

NOTE: Seven minutes is only approx. Frosting should be cooked until thick enough to pile well.

Variations:

Brown Sugar Frosting: Substitute 1 c. brown sugar for white sugar, use 2 tbs. water in place of 3 tbs. Omit corn syrup or cream of tartar.

Fruit and Nut Frosting: Add 1/2 c. either nuts, figs, dates, or raisins, or a combination.

Coconut Frosting: Coconut may be mixed with frosting or sprinkled on top.

 # Candy

On a long, winter Sunday afternoon the children and I, or one alone, may stir up a batch of candy. Come Christmas time we try a variety of recipes.

MOLASSES FUDGE

1½ c. granulated sugar	1/8 t. salt
½ c. molasses	¼ t. cream tartar
½ c. fresh milk	2 tb. butter

Cook sugar, molasses, milk and salt over low heat. Add cream of tartar, stirring until mixture forms a soft ball (236°). Remove from fire, add butter and cool. Beat until firm. Pour into greased pan, cool. Cut into squares. This fudge is rich in vitamin "D", which replaces wasted energy. Give it to the children, they will enjoy it.

BUTTER SCOTCH

1 c. sugar	2 tb. boiling water
¼ c. molasses	1 tb. vinegar
½ c. butter	1 t. vanilla

Mix all ingredients, except vanilla, in saucepan and boil until brittle. Add vanilla; pour into pans. Cut into squares before it is hard.

CREAM CARAMELS

1 c. cream	2 tb. flour
1 c. light syrup	2 tb. cornstarch
¾ c. sugar	1 t. vanilla
¼ c. butter	

Put syrup, sugar, and half of the cream into a saucepan and stir constantly until it boils. Add the rest of the cream slowly. Do not let boiling cease. Cook until a soft ball (236°) forms in water. Add the flour, cornstarch, and butter, creamed together, and continue to cook until a firm soft ball (242°) forms in cold water. Turn into buttered tins and mark in squares when cool. Nuts may be added if desired.

PLAIN CARAMELS

1½ c. brown sugar
1 c. corn syrup
1 c. cream, or evapor-
   ated milk

¼ c. butter
1 t. vanilla
½ c. nut meats

Mix ingredients (except vanilla and nutmeats) well. Cook until it forms a hard--not brittle--string in cold water (117°C or 242°F). Stir occasionally at beginning of cooking period, and constantly after mixture begins to caramelize. Add vanilla and nutmeats. Turn into buttered pans and mark in squares when cool.

DIVINITY FUDGE

2½ c. sugar
½ c. corn syrup
½ c. water

2 egg whites
1 c. nuts
1 t. vanilla

Boil sugar, syrup and water until it forms a firm ball (242°) in water. Beat whites 'til stiff peaks form. Pour half of syrup over eggs, beating constantly. Boil half 'til forms hard ball (250°). Pour on rest of mixture. Add vanilla and nuts. Beat 'til mixture starts to lose its gloss. Pour into buttered pans. Cut into squares when cool.

FUDGE

1½ c. sugar
½ c. milk
2 tb. corn syrup or honey
2 tb. butter

1 sq. chocolate
1 t. vanilla
½ t. salt
½ c. nuts--if desired

Bring sugar, milk, and corn syrup to a boil. Add chocolate and boil to 236°F, or to a soft ball stage, stirring occasionally. Remove from stove, add butter, and cool to a lukewarm temperature. Add flavoring and beat until it begins to thicken and loses its high gloss. Add nuts and salt and pour in pan lined with oiled paper.
NOTE: Use less salt if nuts are omitted. More chocolate may be added for a dark and highly flavored candy.

DATE LOAF

3 c. brown sugar
1 c. milk or cream
1 c. chopped dates

1 c. nuts
1 t. vanilla

Boil sugar and milk 'til it forms a soft ball (236°) in cold water; then add nuts and dates. Boil a while longer; add vanilla. Set in a pan of cold water. Beat and pour out on wet cloth--mold into a roll and let cool. Cut off slices as you serve it.

CHOP SUEY CANDY

4 c. sugar
4 c. light corn syrup
1 pt. sweet cream
¼ c. butter
2 c. coarsely chopped
   walnuts

1 lb. lightly toasted coconut
1 lb. coarsely chopped dates
1 c. whole candied cherries
1 slice candied pineapple
1 c. cut marshmallows

Place sugar, syrup, cream and butter in pan. Mix until sugar is dissolved. Boil until 240°. Cool to lukewarm (116°). Beat until creamy. Add and knead in the remaining ingredients. Shape into rolls 1 1/2" in diameter. Ripen several weeks. Slice candy when ready to serve. (Large recipe.)

POTATO CANDY

1/3 c. mashed potatoes
1¾ c. powdered sugar

1 t. vanilla
2 c. flaked coconut

Mix ingredients thoroughly. Shape into desired balls. Place in refrigerator until very cold. Roll candy in melted German or semi-sweet chocolate.

NOTE: Be creative--experiment with various flavors and shapes, omitting chocolate.

"How sweet are God's words to my taste! Yes, sweeter than honey to my mouth."   Psa. 119:103

PEANUT BRITTLE

2 lbs. sugar	1½ lbs. raw peanuts (Spanish)
1 lb. corn syrup	1 heaping t. soda
3 oz. butter	2/3 pt. water
1 t. vanilla	

Put sugar, syrup and water in large kettle. Boil until it starts to brown, drop butter in center then pour peanuts around it. Boil until peanuts are roasted (stirring constantly). Remove, add vanilla, stir. Then just before pouring add soda dissolved in tsp. of cold water. Mix thoroughly. Pour on cold buttered marble slab. Spread it thin. (Buttered cookie sheets may be used instead of slab. Cools more slowly.)

POPCORN BALLS

2 c. sugar	2 tb. molasses
½ c. corn syrup	1 tb. butter
1 t. salt	Popped corn
1 c. water	

Mix all ingredients except corn and boil to 250°F, or to a hard ball stage. Pour over corn, stir well, and mold.
NOTE: Molasses may be omitted and white corn syrup used, with coloring added if desired.

PUFFED RICE CANDY

2 c. sugar	2 tb. butter
1 c. water	Puffed rice (3½ oz.)
4 tb. molasses	½ c. nuts (optional)
2 t. vinegar	

Combine all ingredients except rice. Cook until it forms a hard ball (265°) when dropped in cold water. Add puffed rice and mix thoroughly. Pour onto buttered pans. Cool. Cut in squares.

"Pleasant words are as an honeycomb, sweet to the soul, and health to the bones." Prov. 16:24

Cereals

Hot cereals are a must for breakfast--the year around. <u>Whole wheat</u> tops it as the favorite.

COOKED CEREAL

Fix rolled oats, cream of wheat, or any cereal according to recipe on box. Add 1/3 c. raisins a few minutes before serving. Cook with milk intead of water, over low flame.

<u>Variations</u>:
1) Serve cereals with dates, figs, or any dried fruit.
2) Brown sugar, or honey, or sorghum may be used for sweetening.

WHOLE WHEAT CEREAL

Thoroughly clean and wash 1 c. whole grained wheat. Soak overnight in cold water. Add 1/2 t. salt and boil until soft (approx. 4 hours). Stir frequently. Serve hot with milk and sugar.

GRAPE-NUTS

2 c. buttermilk, or sour milk   3½ c. graham flour
1/3 c. dark syrup   1 t. salt
1 t. soda

Sift together dry ingredients. Add syrup and buttermilk. Beat until smooth. Spread dough on greased pans, about 1/4-inch thick. Bake at 375⁰ for 15 minutes, or until crisp and golden brown. Cool. Grind through a food chopper. Keep crisp in airtight container.

"Better is little with the fear of the Lord than great treasure with lots of trouble therewith." Prov. 15:16

 Cookies

Our cookie jar doesn't stay filled for long. But drop cookies and soft cookies are favorites.

RAISIN BARS

1 c. raisins	1 t. soda
1 c. water	1 t. cinnamon
½ c. oil	1 t. allspice
1 egg (beaten)	½ t. cloves
1 1/3 c. flour	½ t. nutmeg
1 c. sugar	¼ t. salt

Bring raisins and water to boil, add oil and cool to lukewarm. Add the remainder of ingredients, mix thoroughly and bake in moderate oven at 350°, for 40-45 minutes. Bake in 8" square pan. Sprinkle with confectioners sugar upon removing from oven. When cool cut in bars 1"x4".

OATMEAL DROP COOKIES

2 eggs, well beaten	¼ t. cloves
1 c. sugar	½ t. cinnamon
¾ c. shortening--softened	½ c. raisins
2 c. flour	2/3 c. sour milk
½ t. soda	2 c. rolled oats
½ t. salt	

Combine eggs, sugar, and shortening. Beat well. Add sifted dry ingredients, milk, raisins, and oats. Mix thoroughly. Drop from a teaspoon on greased tin. Bake in a moderate oven 350°, about 15 min.

" O taste and see that the Lord is good." Psa. 34:8a

DROP COOKIES

2/3 c. shortening
1 1/3 c. sugar
1 egg
¼ c. milk
2 c. flour

2 t. baking powder
¼ t. salt
1 t. vanilla
½ t. lemon

Cream sugar and shortening. Add egg, mix thoroughly. Add
flavoring. Measure dry ingredients, sift together and add to
mixture. Add milk. Mix thoroughly. Dough should drop off
spoon very nicely. Bake at 350⁰, 12-15 min.
Variations: To dry ingredients add 1/2 c. chopped nuts; or
1/2 c. chopped raisins; or 1 1/2 c. chopped dates; or 1 1/2
c. coconut.

COFFEE COOKIES

2 c. brown sugar
1 c. shortening
½ c. water
½ c. coffee (diffusion)
1 t. baking powder

1 t. soda
2 eggs
1 c. raisins
4 c. flour
Vanilla

Cream sugar and shortening, add water and coffee (to which the
soda has been added). Add beaten eggs, flour which has been
sifted with baking powder. Flavor with vanilla. Drop on cookie
sheet, bake in hot oven. Nuts may be added.

SNICKERDOODLES

Mix thoroughly...
    1 c. shortening (part butter)
    1½ c. sugar
    2 eggs
Sift together and stir in...
    2 3/4 c. sifted flour
    2 t. cream of tarter

1 t. soda
¼ t. salt

Roll into balls the size of small walnuts. Roll in mixture of 2
tbs. sugar and 2 t. cinnamon. Place 2" apart on ungreased
baking sheet. Bake until lightly browned...but still soft.
(These cookies puff up at first, then flatten out.)
    Temperature: 400⁰ Time: 8-10 min.

SUGAR CAKES

2 c. sugar
¾ c. shortening
1 c. buttermilk
  (or sour milk)
3 eggs

Approx. 4¼ c. flour
2 t. baking powder
1 t. soda
1 t. salt
1 t. vanilla

Cream shortening and sugar. Add eggs, mix thoroughly. Add vanilla. Measure dry ingredients, sift together and add alternately with buttermilk. Drop on greased cookie sheet. Bake at 350° for 12-15 minutes.

NUT AND FRUIT COOKIES

1 c. shortening
  (half butter)
1 c. brown sugar
½ c. molasses
3 eggs
3½ c. flour
½ t. salt
1 t. soda

1½ tb. hot water
Grated rind ½ orange
1 t. cinnamon
½ c. chopped raisins
¾ c. candied fruit
½ c. chopped nuts
½ t. vanilla

Cream shortening and sugar together. Add eggs and beat until fluffy. Add molasses. Measure dry ingredients. Dissolve soda in hot water and add to creamed mixture. Add half of sifted dry ingredients and mix thoroughly. Fold in chopped fruits, nuts, flavoring, remaining flour, and stir until well blended. Drop by teaspoonfuls onto a greased baking sheet. Bake at 350° for 15 minutes.

COCONUT COOKIES

1 c. shortening
  (half butter)
2 c. light brown sugar
2 eggs
3 c. flour
½ t. salt

1 t. soda
1 t. cream of tartar
2 tb. water
2 c. grated coconut
1½ t. vanilla

Cream shortening and sugar together. Add eggs, water and vanilla and beat until fluffy. Measure dry ingredients. Sift into mixture, and beat until smooth. Add grated coconut and blend into mixture. Drop by teaspoonfuls onto greased baking sheet. Bake at 350° for 10 to 12 min. or until lightly browned.

RAISIN-FILLED COOKIES

1 c. butter
2 c. sugar
2 eggs, beaten
2 t. vanilla
6 c. sifted flour

1 t. baking powder
1 t. baking soda
1 t. salt
2/3 c. sour milk or
  buttermilk

Filling:

1½ c. sugar
3 tb. flour
½ c. chopped nuts

3 c. seedless raisins,
  ground
1½ c. water

Cream butter with sugar. Add eggs and vanilla. Sift dry ingredients together. Add alternately to creamed mixture with milk.
Mix well. Cover and chill overnight. Filling: Stir and simmer
ingredients until thickened. Cool. Roll out cooky dough, a por-
tion at a time, on a floured board or pastry cloth. Cut with a 3"
round cutter. If you do not have one use the end of a washed,
empty No. 2 size can. Put a spoonful of filling in the center of
one circle. Top with another. Moisten edges with a little water
and press firmly together with tines of a fork. Bake in a moderately hot oven, 375º, 17-20 minutes.

OLD-FASHIONED SOUR-CREAM COOKIES

¼ c. butter
2 eggs, beaten
1½ c. sugar
2½ c. sifted flour
¼ t. salt

1 t. baking soda
1 c. sour cream
1 t. nutmeg
Raisins (optional)

Cream butter with sugar until light and fluffy. Add well-beaten
eggs. Stir mixture until well blended and pale in color. Sift
the flour with salt and baking soda. Add to creamed mixture
alternately with the sour cream. Flavor with nutmeg and mix
well. Drop by tablespoonfuls onto your baking sheets. Allow
several inches between the cookies. Place a large, soft, seed-
ed raisin in the center of each, if you like. Bake in a moderately
hot oven, 375º, 12-15 minutes.
NOTE: Mix nutmeg with several tablespoons of sugar and
       sprinkle on top of cookies before baking.

SOFT GINGER COOKIES

1¼ c. butter
1/3 c. brown sugar
1½ c. molasses
1 egg
2 t. ginger
1½ t. cinnamon

1½ t. allspice
5 c. sifted flour
½ c. boiling water
4 t. baking soda
½ t. salt

Cream butter and sugar together. Add molasses and egg. Mix until very well blended. Sift spices and 2 c. flour together. Add to creamed mixture alternately with boiling water. Add another cup flour and mix well. Sift the remaining 2 c. flour with the baking soda and salt. Add and stir very thoroughly. Drop by tablespoons on baking sheets. Bake in moderately hot oven, 375°, for about 10 minutes.

CARROT COOKIES

½ c. shortening
1 c. brown sugar
½ c. granulated sugar
1 egg
1 c. cooked carrots, mashed

2 c. flour
½ t. salt
1½ t. baking powder
¾ c. raisins
1 t. vanilla

Cream shortening and sugar. Add vanilla and cooked carrots (mashed and cooled). Sift together dry ingredients. Add dry ingredients. Beat until smooth. Add chopped raisins. Mix. Drop by teaspoonfuls onto a greased baking sheet. Bake 375°, 10-12 minutes.

Orange Frosting

Spread following orange frosting over warm cookies: Rub 1 t. soft butter into 1 1/2 c. powdered sugar. Add juice and grated rind of 1 orange. Beat until smooth.

PINEAPPLE COOKIES

½ c. shortening
½ c. brown sugar
½ c. white sugar
1 egg
2 c. flour
¼ t. salt

½ t. soda
1 t. baking powder
½ c. crushed pineapple, drained
1 t. vanilla or lemon extract
½ c. shredded coconut

Cream shortening and sugar. Add egg and flavoring and beat until fluffy. Drain pineapple and add to creamed mixture. Sift dry ingredients together. Gradually add to mixture. Mix thoroughly. Fold in shredded coconut. Drop by teaspoonfuls onto greased baking sheet. Bake at 375° for 10-12 min.

Desserts

Dessert often consists of either fresh or cooked fruit.   Milk
puddings rate a close second.

BAKED APPLES

6 large red baking apples	1 t. cinnamon
1 tb. butter	½ c. water
6 tb. sugar	½ c. dark molasses or sorghum

Wash apples.   Remove cores, leaving apples whole.   Place in
a buttered flat baking dish. In the center of each apple put 1/2 t.
butter and 1 tb. sugar and cinnamon mixture.   Combine water
and molasses and pour over apples.   Bake at 350° for approx.
45 min.   Baste occasionally.   (Raisins may be added to apples.)

FRUIT COBBLER

2 c. sliced apples	1 tb. butter
½ c. sugar	Biscuit dough (p.4)
1 t. cinnamon	

Peel and core apples.   Slice into buttered baking dish.   Sprinkle
with sugar and cinnamon.   Dot with butter.   Drop biscuit dough
by spoonfuls on top of apples. Bake at 350°, for 40 min.   Serve
warm with milk.
Variation: Apricots, raspberries, cherries, rhubarb can be
used instead of apples.   More sugar can be added at the table if
desired.

FRUIT TAPIOCA

2 c. fruit	4 tb. minute tapioca
2 c. water	½ to 1 c. sugar

Place ingredients in saucepan.   Put over low flame.   Stir frequently.   Boil until clear. Use tart fruit: apples, apricots,
cherries, rhubarb, pineapple, raspberries.   Three cups orange
juice may be used instead of fruit and water.

TAPIOCA CREAM

2 c. scalded milk
2 tb. minute tapioca
1 egg

1/3 c. sugar
½ t. flavoring
¼ t. salt

Place milk, tapioca and sugar in heavy saucepan. Place over low flame. Bring to a boil and boil about 5 min; stir frequently. Beat egg, pour half of hot mixture slowly over egg, stirring constantly. Return to hot milk, stir. Cook about 1 min. Remove from fire, add flavoring and salt. Chill. (Delicious if cooked with rind of 1 orange. Remove rind when ready to serve.)

CORNSTARCH PUDDING

3¾ tb. cornstarch
6 tb. sugar
3 c. milk

1½ t. vanilla
1/8 t. salt
1 egg (beaten)

Scald milk. Mix dry ingredients, moisten with a small amount of cold milk. Add to hot milk. Stir until mixture thickens. Cook about 5 min. over low flame. Pour half over egg, stirring constantly. Mix with remainder and return to stove for 1 min. Add flavoring.

Variation: Add 1 sq. chocolate or 3 tbs. cocoa to dry ingredients.

BAKED CUSTARD

3 c. milk
6 tb. sugar
3 eggs (slightly beaten)

¾ t. vanilla
¼ t. salt
Few grains nutmeg

Scald milk. Add slowly to egg and sugar, stirring constantly. Add flavoring and salt. Pour into custard cups (or baking dish). Place in pan of warm water and bake in a moderate oven, 350° about 1 hour. Cook until knife thrust in center comes out clean.

BREAD PUDDING

6 slices bread
2 c. milk
3 tb. butter
¼ c. sugar

½ t. salt
3 eggs
1 t. vanilla
½ t. nutmeg

Place day old bread in buttered baking dish. Scald milk. Add butter, sugar and salt. Beat eggs and slowly pour milk over eggs. Mix thoroughly. Add flavoring. Pour mixture over bread. Bake at 350° for 1 hour. Serve warm or cold with milk or lemon sauce.

NOTE: Broken pieces of bread may be used. If hard, pour 1 c.
        boiling water over bread. Cover and steam for 10 min.
        --Substitute brown sugar or molasses for sugar.
        --Add 1/2 c. raisins.

RHUBARB PUDDING

3 c. diced fresh rhubarb   1 c. raw rolled oats
1 c. sugar   1½ c. flour
3 tb. flour   ½ c. butter
1 c. brown sugar   ½ c. other shortening

Combine rhubarb, 1 c. sugar, and 3 tb. flour. Place in greased,
6 x 10 baking dish. Combine brown sugar, oats, flour; then cut
in the butter and shortening. Sprinkle over rhubarb mixture.
Bake at 375° (moderate) for 40 minutes. Serve warm with
cream.

GLORIFIED RICE

2 c. cooked rice   1 t. vanilla
1/3 c. sugar   1 banana
3/4 c. cream (may be whipped)

Cut banana into small squares, thoroughly mix all ingredients.
Chill for at least an hour before serving.

RICE DESSERT

Cook rice in half milk, half water in heavy saucepan. Stir frequently. Just before rice is cooked add raisins. Sweeten with
brown sugar. Serve hot or cold. Sprinkle with cinnamon if desired.

ORANGE CHARLOTTE

1 level tb. gelatine   1 c. sugar
¼ c. cold water   2 tb. lemon juice
½ c. boiling water   1 c. orange juice
Pinch of salt   5 egg whites

Soak gelatine in cold water about 5 min. Dissolve in boiling
water. Add sugar and salt. Add lemon juice, cool slightly.
Add orange juice and pulp. When it begins to thicken add
whites of eggs beaten stiffly. Blend thoroughly.

NOTE: Pineapple, grape, raspberry, apricot or strawberry
        juice, may be substituted for orange juice. 1/2 c.
        stiffly whipped cream may be added and use less whites.

LEMON CHIFFON PUDDING

1½ c. sugar
4½ tb. butter
6 tb. flour
¼ t. salt

¼ c. lemon juice
Grated rind of ½ lemon
4 eggs, separated
1½ c. milk

Combine sugar, butter, flour and salt. Add lemon juice, rind and beaten egg yolks. Beat thoroughly. Add milk and blend into mixture. Fold in stiffly beaten egg whites. Pour into a buttered baking dish and set in a pan of hot water. Bake at 350° for 45 minutes. Serve warm.

COCONUT DELIGHT

1 c. graham cracker crumbs
½ c. moist flaked coconut
½ c. chopped walnuts
4 egg whites

¼ t. salt
1 t. vanilla
1 c. sugar
1 pt. ice cream

Combine graham cracker crumbs, coconut, and nuts. Beat egg whites with salt and vanilla 'til foamy. Gradually add sugar and continue beating 'til egg whites form stiff peaks. Fold graham cracker mixture into white mixture. Spread in well-greased 9" pie plate or 10x6x1 1/2" baking pan. Bake at 350° about 30 min. Cool, cut and serve with scoops of ice cream.

CARAMEL APPLES

4 c. thinly sliced apples
3 tb. butter

½ c. brown sugar
1 c. water

Brown butter in large skillet. Add apples. Turn after a few minutes. Add brown sugar and water. Cover tightly and simmer until apples are tender, (15-20 min.). Serve warm. If desired, serve with cream.

BAKED RICE PUDDING

¼ c. rice
1 qt. milk, scalded
1/3 c. sugar

½ t. salt
1 tb. butter
1 t. vanilla or rind of 1 orange

Wash rice. Add other ingredients and pour into a greased baking dish. Bake at 325° approx. 2 hours or until rice is tender. Stir occasionally, folding in brown layer which forms on top. Serve while warm.

QUICK FREEZER ICE CREAM

For 1 gallon freezer:
    1 qt. (thin) cream
    2 qts. milk
    2 c. sugar

½ t. salt
6 eggs
1 tb. vanilla
¼ t. lemon

Combine milk and cream. Add sugar, salt and vanilla and stir until well blended. Beat eggs and add to mixture. Pour into freezer can. Use finely chopped ice, 5 parts ice to 1 part salt. Turn crank slowly for first 6 min., then turn rapidly. Add more ice and salt as needed.

Variations: Use 2 c. less milk. When partly frozen add:
    (1) 1 c. mashed bananas and 1 c. crushed pineapple;
    (2) 2 c. strained black raspberries;
    (3) 1 c. mashed bananas and 1 c. grapenuts;
    (4) 2 c. mashed fresh peaches;
    (5) 2 c. mashed fresh strawberries.

LEMON SHERBET

6 tb. lemon juice
2 tb. orange juice
1 c. sugar
Pinch of salt

2 egg whites
½ c. cream
3/4 c. water

Heat sugar and water to boiling and boil 10 min. Cool. Strain fruit juices and mix them. Keep cool; add cool syrup to juices and pour into tray; freeze firm. Then put mixture into ice-cold mixing bowl and beat light--then add stiffly beaten egg whites and cream. Blend thoroughly and return to freezer. Again freeze firm before serving.

FROZEN FRUIT SALAD

2 oranges
1 apple
1 c. pineapple
½ lb. California grapes
1 c. cooked pears

1 c. diced cantelope
1 c. whipped cream
2 tb. sugar
3 tb. salad dressing

Peel oranges and apple. Cut grapes in half lengthwise and remove seeds. Chop fruit. Mix and put into freezer trays. Whip cream, add sugar and salad dressing. When fruit is partially frozen, remove from trays. Blend with cream. Return to trays. Freeze.

NOTE: Serve on lettuce leaf with toasted cheese sandwiches for a delicious lunch!

Egg and Cheese Dishes

Eggs provide our main breakfast dish...all year long...and very frequently for Saturday supper.

Cheese dishes are always quickly gobbled up.

SCRAMBLED EGGS

6 eggs
1/3 c. rich milk
2 tb. butter

¼ t. salt
Dash of pepper

Stir eggs slightly with fork. Add salt and milk. Stir. Brown butter in skillet. Add egg mixture. Cook at medium temperature. Stir frequently until cooked (Moist, not dry.) Serve immediately.

Instead of butter, dice bacon, fry and pour eggs into skillet.

TORTILLA

½ onion
3 tb. fat
4 eggs

1 c. cooked potatoes
Dash of pepper
¼ t. salt

Slightly brown minced onion in fat. Use medium sized skillet. Add sliced potatoes. Brown. Stir eggs slightly with fork. Add seasoning. Pour onto potatoes. Cover. Cook on low heat until eggs congeal. Flip over entire omlette. Brown. Serve immediately.

Variation: Substitute cooked peas, or finely chopped cooked spinach for the potatoes.

"A merry heart maketh a cheerful countenance."

Prov. 15:13a

FRENCH TOAST

8 slices bread   ¼ t. salt
4 eggs   2 c. milk

Slightly beat eggs, add salt and milk. Dip slice of bread in egg
mixture and fry in skillet. Use meat fryings. Serve hot with
honey, sorghum or maple syrup.

PICKLED EGGS

Hard-boil eggs. Peel. Bring to boil pickled red-beet juice.
(Save the juice when you serve the beets. Store in refrigerator
until you have the amount needed.) Combine whole eggs and
liquid in jar. Place in refrigerator. Serve after several days.

BAKED MACARONI AND CHEESE

2 c. macaroni   1½ c. soft cheese
6 c. boiling water   ½ c. bread crumbs
1 t. salt

Cook macaroni in salt water and drain. Add cheese to white
sauce, cook until melted. Place macaroni in greased casserole. Pour on white sauce. Sprinkle crumbs over top and
bake at 350° for 30 minutes.

White Sauce

3 tb. butter   1 t. salt
2 tb. flour   2 c. milk

Melt fat in heavy saucepan. Add flour and seasoning and stir
until well blended. Slowly add milk, stirring constantly until
a smooth paste is formed.
Medium White Sauce: Use 4 tb. butter and 4 tb. flour.

CHEESE AND JELLY STRATA

Arrange 4 slices of day old bread in 8" square baking pan.
Cover each slice with cheese. Cover with 4 more slices of
bread. Combine 4 beaten eggs, 1 1/2 c. milk, 1/2 t. salt, 1/4
t. mustard and a dash of pepper. Pour over sandwiches. Let
stand 1 hour. Turn sandwiches after 30 minutes. Bake at 325°,
45 minutes. Let stand a few minutes. Top with jelly or jam.

COTTAGE CHEESE

1½ gal. sour milk   1 tb. sugar
1 t. salt   ½ c. cream

Heat milk slowly to about 115°. Drain in a cloth bag or strainer. When dry, crumble curds fine. Add seasonings and cream. Mix thoroughly. Serve with apple butter or molasses.

CREAMED EGGS

6 eggs   1½ t. salt
6 tb. butter or margarine 3 c. milk
6 tb. flour   Dash of pepper

Hard boil eggs. Peel. Melt butter in heavy saucepan. Add flour and seasoning. Stir until well blended. Slowly add milk, stirring constantly. Cook until smooth. Chop eggs and add to sauce. Serve on toast.

HOT CHEESE SANDWICHES

For one sandwich:

½ c. cheese sauce   1 slice bread
1 slice bacon   Tomato slices

Prepare Medium White Sauce (p. 29) to which cheese has been added. Fry bacon crisp. Toast bread. Place bread on serving plate. Cover with tomato slices. Add bacon and pour hot sauce over all. Serve immediately.

"She that hath friends must show herself friendly."
Prov. 18:24

 Fish

We have never been fish fans! But do include this "brain food" in the menu once a week.

FRESH FISH

Clean. Roll in corn meal. Salt to flavor and fry to golden brown.

FILLET

Cut into serving pieces. Dip in beaten egg to which salt has been added, then roll in cracker crumbs. Fry slowly until golden brown.

NOODLE AND TUNA CASSEROLE

1/3 lb. noodles	1 c. canned tuna
1½ qt. boiling water	One 10½ oz. can mushroom soup
1½ t. salt	¾ c. buttered bread cubes
1 can peas	

Cook noodles in salt water until tender. Drain. Flake the tuna with a fork. Mix with noodles, peas and mushroom soup. Turn into a greased baking dish. Sprinkle with bread and bake at 350° for 40 minutes. Serves 6.

SALMON CAKES

2 c. canned salmon	½ t. salt
1 egg	¾ c. cracker crumbs
½ c. milk	

Flake salmon. Add remaining ingredients. Mix thoroughly. Shape into "cakes" and fry until golden brown.

SALMON LOAF

2 c. canned salmon	2 tb. minced green or red
2 c. soft bread crumbs	peppers
1 c. milk	1 t. salt
2 eggs, beaten	2 tb. butter

Flake the fish. Combine all ingredients. (Including liquid from salmon.) Shape in a loaf and bake in greased baking pan at 350°, 40 minutes.

Jams and Jellies

Honey, sorghum and syrup are favorite spreads for homemade bread. We serve jams and jellies occasionally, and when entertaining.

STRAWBERRY PRESERVES

4 c. berries
2 tb. vinegar
4 c. sugar

Boil berries and vinegar for 3 min. Add sugar and boil 10 min. Pour into jelly glasses. Seal with paraffin.

ORANGE MARMALADE

3 large oranges
1 lemon

3 qts. water
4 lbs. sugar

Wash oranges and lemon. Squeeze to remove the juice. Grind the rinds. Mix juice and rind together. Add water and let stand overnight. In the morning, bring to a boil and cook 1 hour. Add sugar; stir until dissolved. Cook rapidly until thick. Pour into jars and seal.

PEAR HONEY

8 lbs. pears
8 lbs. sugar
2 c. crushed pineapple

Wash pears. Remove cores. Grind pears in food chopper. Place in large cooking pan. Add sugar and pineapple and stir until sugar is dissolved. Bring to a boil and cook until thick (about 20 min.). Stir frequently.

CHERRY PRESERVES

3 lbs. red cherries
3 lbs. sugar

Wash, stem and seed cherries. Bring to boiling point, stirring
frequently. Add sugar gradually. Stir. Cook preserves 25
minutes. Add a few drops of red coloring. Pour into bowl.
Let stand 12 hours. Put into jars and cover with paraffin.

APPLE JELLY

3 c. apple juice
3 c. sugar

Save peelings and cores when fixing apples. (Red variety, not
green or yellow.) Put in a saucepan. Add enough water until
it can be seen through pieces of peeling. Cover and cook
slowly until peelings are soft. Pour into a bag and suspend
over a bowl; let hang until juice no longer drips; do not
squeeze bag. Measure juice and bring to a boil. Add sugar
gradually and cook rapidly until it begins to thicken. When
the last 2 drops on the spoon run together and "sheet off,"
remove jelly from stove. Pour into hot jelly glasses and
cover with paraffin.

APPLE BUTTER

2 qts. apple cider
4 qts. apples
4 c. sugar, (or 3 c. white
    and 1 c. brown sugar)

1 t. powdered cinnamon or
    ¼ t. oil of cinnamon
    (if desired.)

Boil the cider until it is reduced to 1 qt. Pare apples, core
and slice in thin pieces. Add apples to cider and cook slowly
until the mixture begins to thicken. Stir frequently. Then
add sugar, syrup (and cinnamon). Cook until a sample, when
cooled on a plate, is of a good consistency to spread.

DULCE DE LECHE

Place unopened can of condensed milk in teakettle, or pan of
water (completely immersed). Boil for 1 1/2 hours. Cool.
Open can at both ends. Remove contents. Keep in tight container. Makes a delicious spread for bread.

Meats

Meat (or substitute), potatoes, salad, a vegetable--either buttered or creamed, and fruit...that's a typical meal. But plenty of each!

TALLERINES

1½ lbs. lean meat	1 minced onion
1/3 c. cooking oil	2 c. tomato juice
Salt to taste	2 diced carrots
2 cloves garlic	1 c. water
½ t. oregano	Grated cheese
1 tb. minced parsley	8 oz. pkg. wide noodles

Cube meat in 1" pieces. Brown in oil. Add seasoning, tomato juice, carrots and water. Simmer 2 hours. In kettle of boiling salt water, add noodles. Cook until tender (approx. 15 min.); drain. Arrange on large platter, cover with meat sauce, and sprinkle with grated cheese.

MEAT BALLS IN TOMATO JUICE

1 lb. hamburger	1/8 t. pepper
1 c. bread crumbs	¼ c. milk
1 or 2 eggs	1 pt. tomato juice
¾ t. salt	1 large onion
Dash of garlic salt or fresh garlic clove	

Mix ingredients well, (except tomato juice and onion). Shape into 8 balls. Brown in large skillet. Add tomato juice and minced onion. Simmer for approximately 1 hour.

"My meat is to do the will of Him that sent me." John 4:34

MEAT LOAF

1½ lbs. hamburger
1 c. soft bread crumbs
1 c. milk
½ c. tomato juice
1 onion, minced

Dash of garlic salt
1 or 2 eggs, beaten
1 t. salt
1/8 t. pepper
6 strips bacon

Combine all ingredients except bacon. Form into a loaf and place in baking dish. Place strips of bacon on top. Bake at 375° for 1 hour.

Variation: 1 lb. hamburger and 1/2 lb. ground fresh pork, or 1/2 lb. ground cured ham.

STUFFED PORK CHOPS

6 large pork chops
1 t. salt
Bread dressing

Fry chops in a little fat until slightly brown. Salt and place in a roasting pan. Cover with bread dressing. Add 1 cup hot water and the fat in which chops were fried. Cover and bake slowly for 1 hour.

Bread Dressing

1 qt. soft bread crumbs
3 eggs
2 c. milk
1 tb. chopped parsley

1 tb. chopped celery
1 t. minced onion
1 t. salt
3 tb. fat

Beat eggs. Add milk. Pour liquid over bread crumbs. Add remaining ingredients and mix well. Pour into greased casserole. Bake at 350° about 30 minutes.

Use chicken fat when serving with roast chicken.

BAKED WHOLE HAM

1 cured ham
2 c. pickled peach juice

cloves
1 c. brown sugar

Cover ham with water and cook until done. Slightly cool. Remove skin and fat. Place in roaster. Rub in brown sugar. Stick with whole cloves. Add peach juice. Bake at 350°, basting with juice every 10 min. Allow to brown slightly.

HAM LOAF

1 lb. fresh ham (shoulder) ½ c. bread crumbs
½ lb. cured ham ½ c. milk
1 egg

Grind meat. Mix ingredients. Make into a loaf--add 1/2 c.
water. Bake 45 minutes at 375°. Serves 6.

LIVER 'N ONIONS

Quickly brown slices of liver on one side. Salt. Turn. Cover
with thinly chopped onions. Add a dash of salt. Cover and
brown at low temperature. When tender serve immediately.

QUISO

Meat sauce 1 c. diced raw potatoes
1½ c. uncooked rice 2 c. water
1 c. fresh peas 1 t. salt

Prepare meat as for Tallerines (p.34). At the last hour add rice
and water. Cook 20 min. Add remaining ingredients. Cook
over low flame until vegetables are done. Add more water as
needed. (If cooked peas are used, add only to heat thoroughly.)
Variation: Prepare meat sauce. Add 4 c. water and 1 1/2 c.
cornmeal. Cook slowly for 1 hour. Stir frequently.

MEAT GRAVY

½ lb. hamburger 1 c. water
¾ t. salt 1 c. milk
2 tb. flour

Brown hamburger in large skillet. (If lean add 2 tb. fat.) Add
salt, dash of pepper. Add flour. Stir. Let brown slightly.
Add water and milk. Stir constantly. Boil about 5 minutes.
Serve with potatoes boiled in jackets.
Variations: Substitute 1 package chipped dried beef, browned
in butter; or 1/2 lb. sausage (browned).

CHICKEN AND DUMPLINGS

1 chicken (preferably old
   hen)
1½ t. salt
1 small onion
2 tb. chopped celery leaves
2 bay leaves

For Dumplings:
2 c. flour
½ t. salt
4 t. baking powder
1 egg, beaten
2/3 c. milk

Cut chicken into serving pieces. Cover with water and cook slowly until almost tender. Add finely chopped onion, celery leaves and seasoning. Cook 15 min. and then add the dumplings to the boiling broth and meat.

To make dumplings: Sift dry ingredients together. Add beaten egg and milk. Stir until well blended. Drop dough from a teaspoon into boiling chicken. Cover tightly. Cook 12 more minutes. Do not uncover until ready to serve.

CHICKEN CASSEROLE

2 c. diced cooked chicken
2 c. soft bread cubes
1 tb. minced parsley
1 t. salt
1 tb. minced celery leaves

¼ t. pepper
2 eggs, beaten
1½ c. chicken broth
1½ c. milk

Place half of bread cubes in a greased casserole. Then add chicken and seasoning. Place remaining bread cubes on top. Beat eggs. Add milk and broth. Pour over mixture. Bake at 350° for 45 minutes. Serves 6.

CHICKEN 'N RICE

1 chicken
1/3 c. cooking oil
2 clove garlic
2 tb. chopped parsley
½ t. oregano

2 carrots
1 onion
2 c. tomato juice
1 t. salt
2. c. rice

Brown chicken in oil. Add seasoning, finely chopped carrots and onion. Simmer 1 hour, (or until tender). Remove chicken. Add washed rice. Brown in sauce, to which more oil has been added (if necessary). Add 1 cup water, cover and steam for 35 minutes. Stir occasionally. Add meat for final 20 minutes.

CREAMED CHICKEN

2 c. diced chicken
1 c. milk
1 c. chicken broth or gravy
½ t. salt

2 tb. chicken grease or butter
2 tb. flour
Dash of pepper
1 t. minced celery leaves

Melt grease in heavy saucepan. Add flour and seasonings. Add
liquids and stir until smooth. Add chicken and heat thoroughly.
Serve on hot Biscuits (p. 4).

(A good way to use the leftover roast chicken, picked off the
bones, and the leftover gravy.)

CHICKEN SUPREME

1 fryer chicken
¼ lb. butter or margarine

Salt to taste
2 c. bread crumbs

Cut chicken into serving pieces. Melt butter in shallow pan,
keep warm. Salt the chicken to taste; dip each piece in melted
butter, then roll in bread crumbs. Place on buttered shallow
pan (or cookie sheet). Bake at 325° for 1 hr. Reduce heat to
300° and bake 25 min. longer (or until tender).

SWISS STEAK

2 lbs. round steak (1" thick)
½ c. flour
3 tb. fat
1½ t. salt

1 onion, minced
¼ t. pepper
3 c. cooked tomatoes, or tomato juice

Pound flour into steak. Quickly brown both sides in fat. Add
salt, pepper and onion. Pour tomatoes over meat. Cover.
Simmer 1 1/2 hours.

CHICKEN AND NOODLES

1 stewing hen
1 small onion
1 tb. minced parsley

2 t. salt
½ lb. noodles

Cook chicken with onion and parsley until tender. Remove
meat from bones. Return meat to broth; should be about 1 qt.
broth--add water if necessary. Bring to boil. Add salt and
noodles. Boil 5 min., stirring occasionally. Cover. Reduce
heat to simmer. Leave on burner for 30 min. Do not remove
cover until ready to serve.

ROAST CHICKEN

1 chicken
2 t. salt
½ c. water

Rub chicken with salt. Place in roaster. Add water. Cover.
Bake at 350° until tender (allow 30 min. per pound). Baste
every 15 min. If crisp skin is desired, leave uncovered the
last 30 min. Remove chicken, and make gravy from broth.

<u>Giblets</u>: Boil giblets in 1 c. water until soft. Cool. Chop into
small pieces. Add with broth and 4 tb. drippings from
roaster pan to Dressing (p. 35).

BROILED WIENERS

6 wieners
6 slices bacon
Cheese
Catsup

Slice wieners lengthwise, do not cut in two. Place cheese in
slit. Wrap bacon slice around wieners and fasten with a tooth-
pick. Place in broil pan. Quickly brown bacon on bottom side.
Turn. Broil at medium heat until bacon is crisp. Pour catsup
over wieners a few minutes before ready to serve.

*"Never refuse to extend your hospitality to strangers--
sometimes men have entertained angels unawares."*
Heb. 13:2

Pickles and Relishes

Our pickle shelf very quickly resembles "Old Mother Hubbard's cupboard." We could eat them twice daily.

LIME WATER CHIPS

7 lbs. cucumbers, slice 1/8". Cover with 2 gal. water and 2 c. household lime. Soak in lime 24 hours. Rinse well. Let stand 3 hrs. in cold water. Drain well--cover with this cold mixture-leave set 8-10 hours, or overnight:

2 qts. vinegar	1 tb. mixed spices
4½ lbs. sugar (9 c.)	2 tb. whole cloves
1 tb. mustard seed	1 tb. salt
1 tb. celery seed	4 small sticks cinnamon

Next morning boil pickles in syrup for 35 min. Can hot and seal.

CHUNK PICKLE

1 gal. cucumber chunks	1 t. allspice
½ c. salt	1 t. mustard seed
Boiling water to cover	1 t. celery seed
3 c. sugar	½ t. tumeric
3 c. vinegar	2 sticks cinnamon
1 c. water	

Cut medium-sized cucumbers into 1" chunks. Add salt and cover with boiling water. Let stand overnight and drain. Combine remaining ingredients. Bring to a boil and add pickles. When the boiling point has been reached, can and seal.

CUCUMBER SWEET PICKLE (Short Process)

1 gal. cucumbers (4 ¾ lbs.)	2 tb. mixed spices
6 c. sugar	1 c. water
1 c. salt	1½ qts. vinegar

Wash cucumbers and wipe them dry. Dissolve salt in 1 gal. cold water and pour over cucumbers. Let stand 24 hrs. and drain. Puncture each cucumber 3 times with a needle. Combine 1/2 of the sugar, vinegar, water and spices. Simmer liquid for 30 min. Add cucumbers to liquid. Let stand in a jar for 2 days. Drain off the liquid and pack pickles in hot jars. Add remaining sugar to liquid and boil 5 min. Pour over pickles and seal.

BEET PICKLE

3 qts. sliced beets, cooked (or small whole beets)
2 c. vinegar
3 t. salt
2 c. sugar

2 c. water
1 t. whole cloves
3 sticks cinnamon
1 t. mustard seed

Place ingredients in large saucepan. Bring to a boil. Seal in sterilized jars. (Spices may be put into bag and removed when ready to can.) Or powdered spices may be used.

NOTE: This brine--equal parts of water, sugar, vinegar and spices to taste--can also be used for pickling watermelon or cantelope.

PICKLED WATERMELON RIND

7 lbs. rind
1 pt. vinegar
½ t. oil of cloves

2½ lbs. sugar
½ t. oil of cinnamon
1 pt. water

Peel rind, cut into 2" pieces. Soak overnight in salt water. Boil rind in clear water until tender. Drain. Make syrup of sugar, vinegar, cinnamon and cloves and water. Boil and pour over rind. Next morning pour off syrup and reheat. Pour over rind. The third day reheat syrup with rind in it. Put in jars and seal.

CRANBERRY RELISH

1 lb. raw cranberries
3 raw apples
2 oranges
2 c. sugar

½ c. nuts
1 c. crushed pineapple (optional)

Grind cranberries, apples and oranges through coarse blade of food grinder. Use peeling of one orange. Add sugar and let stand 6-8 hours in refrigerator. Add nuts just before serving. Serves 8.

Pies

I prefer baking pies to cakes. The design on the upper crust and the way the edges are pinched together I learned as a small girl by watching Mother. Fruit pies are our first choice.

PASTRY

2 c. flour	1 t. baking powder
2/3 c. shortening	½ t. salt
1/3 c. cold water	

Sift dry ingredients together. Put in mixing bowl. Cut shortening into flour with a pastry blender (or with hands). Add water gradually using only enough to hold pastry together when it is pressed between the fingers. Roll dough into a round ball, handling as little as possible. Roll out on a lightly floured board into a circle 1/8" thick and 1" larger than the diameter of the top of the pan.

FRUIT PIE

3 c. sliced apples	½ t. nutmeg or
3/4 c. sugar	1 t. cinnamon
1 tb. flour	2 tb. butter

Line pie plate with pastry. Fill with thinly sliced apples. Mix sugar, cinnamon and flour. Sprinkle over apples. Dot with butter. Cover with upper crust. Bake in oven 400°, for 45 min.

NOTE: If apples are very juicy, 2 tbs. flour may be mixed with the sugar. Add 1 tb. lemon juice if apples are not tart.

Increase sugar to 1 cup, and flour to 3 tbs. if fresh cherries or berries are used.

STRAWBERRY PIE

Fill baked shell with sweetened crushed strawberries. Cover with halved marshmallows and brown.

SOUR CREAM PIE

1 c. sour cream	1 tb. vinegar
2/3 c. sugar	½ t. nutmeg
2 tb. flour	1 egg, beaten (separately)
1 c. chopped raisins	

Thoroughly mix flour and sugar. Add remaining ingredients, mix, and pour into unbaked pie shell. Bake at 425° for 10 minutes, then 325° for 30-40 minutes.

GREEN TOMATO PIE

3 c. green tomatoes	2 tb. flour
½ c. brown sugar	1 t. cinnamon
½ c. molasses	¼ t. nutmeg
½ c. water	

Slice tomatoes in thin rings. Do not pare. Put in unbaked pastry shell. Combine sugar, flour and spices. Add molasses and water. Pour mixture over tomatoes. Cover with a top crust. Bake at 425° for 15 min., reduce temperature to 375° and continue to bake 30 minutes.

PUMPKIN PIE

1½ c. cooked pumpkin	1 t. cinnamon
2 eggs--beaten	¼ t. allspice
1 c. milk	¼ t. cloves
½ c. sugar	¾ t. salt

Mix dry ingredients, add to pumpkin. Add eggs and milk. Mix well. Pour into unbaked crust. Bake until knife inserted in center comes out clean. Temperature: 425° for 15 minutes, then 350° for 25-30 minutes.

NOTE: 1) Substitute honey or brown sugar for the sugar.
2) Use less spices and add 1/2 c. coconut.

SOUR CREAM PEACH PIE

12 peach halves	3/4 c. sour cream
1 c. sugar	1 t. nutmeg
2 tb. flour	

Arrange peach halves in unbaked crust. Mix sugar, flour and nutmeg. Add cream. Thoroughly mix and pour mixture over peaches. Bake at 425° for 15 min, then continue at 375° for 35 minutes.

LEMON PIE

2 c. water
4 tb. cornstarch
1½ c. sugar
½ t. salt

3 eggs--separated
1½ tb. butter
2 lemons
Rind of one lemon

Bring water to boiling point in saucepan. Thoroughly mix corn-starch, sugar, and salt. Add to boiling water, stirring con-stantly to prevent lumping. Stir until thickened. Cook about 5 min. over low heat. Stir a small amount of the mixture into the slightly beaten egg yolks, return to pan and cook slightly. Stir constantly. Remove from fire. Add butter, lemon juice, and grated rind. Beat thoroughly. Cool. Place in a baked shell, and cover with meringue made from the whites. Bake in a slow oven until delicately colored, 300°, about 20 minutes.

CUSTARD PIE

2 c. milk
3 eggs-slightly beaten
½ c. sugar
¼ t. salt

1 t. vanilla
1/8 t. nutmeg
½ c. shredded coconut

Scald milk. Beat eggs slightly in a bowl large enough to hold all the filling. Mix sugar, salt, vanilla and coconut with the eggs, then add milk gradually, stirring constantly. Pour about 3/4 of the filling into an unbaked crust lightly dusted with flour. Place in oven, add remaining filling, and sprinkle nutmeg on top. Bake until a knife inserted in center of the filling comes out clean. Bake at 425° for 10 min., then 325° for 30 to 40 min.

NOTE: It's best to take out pie just before a perfect test is reached. The heat within will finish the cooking pro-cess.

BUTTERMILK PIE

1 c. sugar
2 c. buttermilk
2 eggs

2 tb. butter
2 tb. flour
1 t. lemon flavoring

Combine sugar and flour. Add beaten eggs, melted butter, milk and flavoring. Pour into unbaked pie crust. Bake at 350° for 35 minutes.

MINCE MEAT PIE

Fill unbaked pie shell with 2 1/2 c. mince meat. Cover with
top crust. Seal edges and bake at 425° for 15 min., continue
at 375° for 35 min.

Mince Meat

¼ bu. apples	2 qts. cider
½ gal. sausage	1 qt. other sweet juices
3 lb. beef	Salt, cinnamon, nutmeg and
2 lb. raisins	allspice to taste
3 lbs. sugar	2 qts. red cherries

Peel and dice apples. Place all ingredients in large container
and boil 30 min. (I like to add cherries at the last minute--
just long enough to thoroughly heat. They retain their red
color.) Can in sterilized jars, or freeze.

COCONUT CREAM PIE

1½ c. milk	Yolks of 3 eggs
1/3 c. sugar	1 tb. butter
¼ t. salt	1½ c. coconut
2 tb. cornstarch	1 t. vanilla

Scald milk in heavy saucepan. Mix together dry ingredients.
Add to milk, stirring constantly. Boil 5 min. Beat egg yolks.
Add half of hot mixture. Stir and return to remaining mixture
in pan. Leave on heat about 1 min. Remove. Add butter,
coconut and vanilla. Mix and pour into baked pie shell. Cover
with meringue made with egg whites and 4 tb. sugar. Brown
in oven.

GRAHAM CRACKER PIE

Crust:	Filling:
16 graham crackers	1 can condensed milk
6 tb. melted butter	Juice of 2 lemons
1 1/3 c. sugar	Grated rind of 1 lemon
1 t. cinnamon	3 egg yolks, beaten
1 tb. flour	¼ t. salt

Combine ingredients for crust. Press 3/4 of it into pie plate.
Combine ingredients for filling. Pour into crust. Beat egg
whites until stiff, add 3 tb. sugar. Spread meringue over top
and sprinkle with remaining graham crumbs. Bake at 350°
until golden brown. Chill in refrigerator before serving.

 Salads

Nine times out of ten our salads have a lettuce base...just chopped...with either a cream or oil dressing.

LETTUCE SALAD

Coarsely cut desired amount of lettuce. Add sour cream dressing (or oil dressing). Serve immediately.

Variation: 1) Add 1/2 c. diced cheese.
2) Add 1 chopped, boiled egg; 1 slice bacon (chopped and browned).

TOSSED SALAD

2 c. chopped lettuce
½ c. sliced carrots
½ c. sliced cucumbers
½ c. sliced celery
1 tomato, chopped
Radish (to taste)

1 small onion, minced
½ t. salt
¼ c. cooking oil
¼ c. vinegar
¼ c. sugar

Place vegetables in large bowl. Just before serving add oil and seasoning. Mix thoroughly.

OIL DRESSING

½ c. cooking oil
½ c. vinegar

1 t. salt
½ c. sugar

Mix ingredients thoroughly. (Can be placed in shaker.) Store in refrigerator. Use amount needed for salads.

CREAM DRESSING

½ c. sour cream
   (or sweet)
¼ c. sugar

½ t. salt
2 tb. vinegar

Mix cream and sugar until sugar is dissolved. Add salt and vinegar. Mix thoroughly.

CABBAGE SLAW

Shred desired amount of cabbage. Add sour cream dressing (or oil dressing). Serve immediately.

Variation: Add 1/2 c. chopped tart apples and 1/2 c. nut meats.

CARROT AND RAISIN SALAD

3 c. shredded carrots	2 tb. sugar
¾ c. raisins	Dash of salt
Juice of 1 lemon	

Thoroughly mix ingredients. Serve immediately.

CUCUMBER SLAW

1 large cucumber	½ c. cream (sour or sweet)
½ t. salt	2 tb. vinegar
¼ c. sugar	

Pare and thinly slice cucumber. Combine cream and seasoning. Mix thoroughly. Add to cucumbers. Let stand several hours in covered dish in refrigerator before serving.

APPLE SALAD

3 c. red apples	½ c. cream (whipped)
1 c. diced celery	3 tb. sugar
½ c. coarsely chopped English walnuts	½ t. vanilla

Wash, core and dice apples. (Do not peel.) Add celery and nuts. Just before serving add whipped cream to which sugar and vanilla have been added. Mix thoroughly.

CARROT & PINEAPPLE SALAD

1 pkg. orange gelatin	1 c. crushed pineapple
1 c. pineapple juice	1½ c. ground raw carrots
1 c. boiling water	½ c. chopped nuts

Dissolve gelatin in hot water and add pineapple juice. Chill. When this begins to thicken, add other ingredients. Pour mixture into a mold and chill until set. Serve on lettuce, with or without mayonnaise.

CABBAGE SALAD

1 pkg. lime gelatin
1 c. pineapple juice
1 c. boiling water

2 c. shredded cabbage
1 c. crushed pineapple

Dissolve gelatin in hot water. Add pineapple juice. Chill.
When it begins to thicken, add other ingredients. Pour into
mold. Chill until set. Serve on lettuce and mayonnaise
if desired.
Variation: Prepare lime gelatin as indicated. Add cabbage and
1/2 c. nut meats, omit pineapple.

MACARONI SALAD

3 c. cooked macaroni
2 hard boiled eggs
1 c. chopped celery
1 c. tuna fish
2 tb. mayonnaise

½ c. cream
  (sour or sweet)
¼ c. sugar
1 t. salt
¼ c. vinegar

Combine all ingredients. Mix thoroughly. Place in serving
dish. Garnish with paprika. Chill in refrigerator several
hours before serving.

DANDELION SALAD

4 c. dandelion
3 eggs, hard boiled
3 slices bacon

Dressing:
2 tbs. flour
1 t. salt
2 tb. sugar
¼ c. vinegar
1½ c. water or milk

Wash and chop dandelion. Cut bacon in pieces and fry crisp.
Mix dry ingredients together. Add liquids and pour into
skillet. Cook until thickened. Cool slightly. Pour over
dandelion. Add chopped eggs. Mix lightly.
Variation: Mix chopped dandelion, eggs and crisp bacon,
1/2 t. salt. Add cream dressing (p. 46). Mix
and serve.

*"Whatever work you may have to do, do everything in the
name of the Lord Jesus."* Col. 3:17

Soups

We serve soup almost daily for lunch during the school year.
Variety is necessary. We prefer homemade soups to bought
soups.

STANDARD SOUP STOCK

2 lb. beef shank (or soup bone)	Cabbage, potatoes, turnips, celery,
2 qts. cold water	carrots, onion, parsley,
1 t. salt	1 ear corn, green beans

Place meat and water in pan. Bring to a boil, and simmer for
4 hrs. or more. Add whole vegetables. Cook about 1/2 to 1
hr. longer. (Remove vegetables--can be served hot with butter.)

STOCK SOUPS

Barley Soup: Soak 1/4 c. pearl barley overnight or for several
hours. Cook in 1 qt. water until tender. Add about 1 qt.
stock.

Rice Soup: Add 1/2 to 2 c. cooked rice to 1 qt. stock.

Alphabet Noodle: Add 1/2 to 2 c. cooked noodles to 1 qt. of
stock.

Vegetable: Any mixture of diced vegetables (cabbage, carrot,
peas, turnips, green beans, celery, potatoes and corn) may
be added to stock.

NOTE: Serve toasted bread sticks or crisp crackers with hot
soups. One-half cup tomato may be added to any of the
soups for color and flavor.

"Better is a meal of soup where love is, than a steak din-
ner and hatred."   Prov. 15:17

VEGETABLE SOUP WITH MEAT

1 soup bone	½ qt. tomatoes
1 onion	½ c. diced celery
3 diced carrots	½ c. shredded cabbage
1 c. peas	1 c. corn
1 c. green beans	1 c. lima beans
2 c. diced potatoes	Salt and pepper

Cook the soup bone in enough water to cover. When tender, remove meat from broth and add diced vegetables (more water if needed) and continue to cook for 20 minutes. Season. (Canned vegetables may be substituted. Add just before serving.)

CHILI SOUP

2 c. kidney beans	2 t. salt
½ qt. tomatoes	¼ t. pepper
2 medium—sized onions	1 t. chili powder
1 lb. hamburger	

Cook beans until soft. Put 2 tb. fat in pan and brown minced onion. Add hamburger and fry until brown. Add tomatoes and browned hamburger to cooked beans. Add seasoning. Simmer together 15 minutes. Add water to obtain desired consistency. Serves 6.

CREAM OF TOMATO SOUP

3 tb. butter	1 tb. sugar
4 tb. flour	1 t. salt
2 c. strained tomatoes	1 qt. milk
1 tb. minced onion	1/8 t. pepper
¼ t. celery salt	

Brown onions in butter. Add tomatoes, salt, and pepper. Mix flour and sugar in shaker, add enough milk to form creamy consistency. Shake. Bring tomatoes to boil and slowly stir in thickening. Boil a few minutes, stirring constantly. Very slowly add remaining milk. Heat (not boil) and serve with cheese crackers. Serves 6. (1/3 cup diced bacon may be substituted for butter.)

CHEESE CRACKERS

Place desired amount of soda crackers on cookie sheet. Place thinly sliced cheese on top. Add a dash of pepper and salt. Broil until slightly brown. Serve immediately.

POTATO SOUP

2 c. diced potatoes
3 c. water
2 tb. butter

1 qt. rich milk
1 onion (optional)
Salt and pepper

Cook potatoes and onion in salt water until tender. Add milk
and butter. Heat (don't boil). Just before serving add 2
chopped hard boiled eggs. Serves 8.

OLD-FASHIONED BEAN SOUP

1½ c. navy beans
½ t. salt
1 qt. milk

1 tb. butter
Dash of pepper
Toasted bread cubes

Add salt to beans and cook until soft. Pour off water. Add
milk, butter, pepper and more salt, if desired. Serve with
toasted bread cubes. Serves 6.

CHICKEN SOUP

3–4 lbs. chicken
2½ qts. water
2½ t. salt
1 celery stick

Parsley
1 small onion
2 bay leaves
1 c. rice

Bring chicken to boil in water. Add celery and seasonings.
Simmer several hours until tender. (Add more water if necessary.) Drain broth into sauce pan. Wash rice. Add to
broth and cook until tender.

BREAD SOUP

8 slices bread
2 qts. whole milk

Fresh berries
Sugar to taste

Cube bread. Put into large bowl. Add milk and desired
amount of sugar. Let stand at least 15 min. before serving.
Each person adds the amount of berries he chooses.
Variation: Mix bread and milk as above. Add salt, instead
of sugar and fruit.

". . .in everything give thanks."   I Thess. 5:18

Vegetables

Vegetables fresh from the garden, served with melted butter, browned butter or creamed, are a treat the entire summer. The garden also supplies frozen vegetables for the winter.

ESCALLOPED ASPARAGUS

Put into a baking dish one layer of cooked asparagus and another layer of hard boiled eggs. Repeat 'til full. Pour 1 c. white sauce over it and grate cheese on top. Bake in moderate oven 'til brown.

ASPARAGUS

Boil in salt water. Just before serving add some cream. Pour over toasted bread cubes in serving dish. Add browned butter.

SCALLOPED CORN

2 c. cooked or canned corn	2 eggs
1 c. milk	3 tb. melted butter
½ t. salt	2/3 c. cracker or bread
Dash of pepper	crumbs

Place corn in greased casserole. Cover with crumbs. Beat eggs, add milk, seasoning and butter. Pour over corn. Bake at 350°, 40 minutes.

BAKED GREEN BEANS

1 qt. cooked green beans	1 t. salt
1 c. tomato soup	½ c. soft cheese
½ c. water or milk	½ c. bread crumbs

Place beans in buttered baking dish. Add cubed cheese. Dilute soup with liquid, add salt. Pour over beans. Cover with crumbs. Bake at 375° for 30 minutes.

NOTE: May be unbaked made in heavy saucepan. Omit bread crumbs.

BAKED BEANS

2 c. navy beans
1½ t. salt
½ c. molasses
1/3 c. pickles (finely chopped)
1 t. mustard

¼ t. ginger
½ c. catsup
1 c. tomato juice
Several slices bacon

Soak beans overnight in cold water. Drain and add 2 qts. fresh
water. Cook slowly until skins burst. Drain and save liquid.
Add molasses, pickles, seasoning, catsup, 1 c. liquid from
beans and tomato juice. Pour into greased baking dish. Add
enough water to cover. Place bacon slices on top of beans.
Bake with cover on for 4 1/2 hrs. at 300°. Remove cover,
bake 30 min. Add water as necessary during cooking process.
Variations: 1) Use canned pork and beans. Slightly reduce
seasoning.
2) Brown sausage balls. Add to beans and omit
bacon.

SAUERKRAUT

Shred cabbage. Pack in glass jars. Add 1 teaspoon salt to each
quart jar. Fill jar with boiling water. Seal tightly. Allow it to
ripen several weeks before using.   Cook with spare ribs or
wieners.

PEAS AND POTATOES

3 c. fresh peas
12 small new potatoes
1½ t. salt

1 c. cream
3 tb. butter

Cook peas and potatoes separately in salt water until soft, and
almost dry. Combine. Add cream and butter. Heat thoroughly.
Do not boil.

SCALLOPED POTATOES

6 c. raw potatoes
4 tb. flour
1½ t. salt

1/8 t. pepper
2½ c. top milk or cream
2 tb. butter

Place a layer of sliced potatoes in buttered baking dish. Sprinkle
with salt, pepper and flour. Dot with butter. Repeat until all ingredients are used. Pour hot milk over potatoes and bake at 350°
for 1 to 1 1/4 hours.   Serves 6.

FRIED RAW POTATOES

2 c. potatoes
1 tb. fat
½ t. salt

Slice potatoes very thin. Add potatoes to meat fat in frying pan.
Sprinkle with salt. Cover. Cook over medium fire until tender
and mealy. Turn occasionally and add more fat as needed during
cooking.

MUSTARD BUTTERED POTATOES

3 lbs. potatoes
1/3 c. butter or margarine
1 t. minced onion
3 tb. chopped parsley

2 t. prepared mustard
1½ t. salt
Few grains pepper

Wash and cook potatoes until tender. Peel and dice. Cook
minced onions until tender, but not brown, in melted butter.
Add parsley and seasoning. Pour over hot diced potatoes. Ex-
cellent served with ham.

VEGETABLE CASSEROLE

1 lb. hamburger
2 c. sliced raw potatoes
1 c. diced carrots
1 c. peas
1 c. lima beans
1 minced onion

1 c. corn
3 cabbage leaves
Salt and pepper to taste
1 tb. flour
2 c. milk

Spread 1/2 lb. hamburger on bottom of baking dish. (Season.)
Add a layer of potatoes and 1/2 of remaining vegetables. Add
salt and pepper to each layer. Spread cabbage leaves over
mixture. Add remaining potatoes and vegetables. Sprinkle
with flour. Spread remaining meat on top and pour milk over
all. Bake at 350⁰ for approx. 2 hours. Use fresh or frozen
vegetables.

FRIED EGGPLANT

1 medium-sized eggplant
1 egg
½ t. salt

½ c. cracker crumbs or flour
¼ c. fat

Pare eggplant and slice in rings 1/4" thick. Salt. Roll in
cracker crumbs (or flour). Fry in hot fat until a golden brown
on both sides.

CREAMED VEGETABLES

1 qt. fresh vegetables	¼ c. milk
1 t. salt	2 t. flour
1/8 t. pepper	2 tb. butter
1 c. cream	

Cook fresh vegetables (peas, corn, lima beans, or green beans)
until almost dry and tender. Add seasoning and cream. When
it boils add paste made of flour and milk. Cook about 2 minutes;
add butter.

Variation: 1) Cook vegetables until tender. Serve with butter, or
3 tb. browned butter.

2) Combine peas and carrots in above recipe.

3) Combine carrots and celery in above recipe.

4) Combine lima beans and corn in above recipe.

CANDIED SWEET POTATOES

6 medium-sized sweet potatoes	1 tb. flour
1 t. salt	8 marshmallows
¾ c. brown sugar	½ c. cream (or top milk)
2 tb. butter	¼ c. chopped nuts

Cook potatoes with skins until soft, but not mushy. Peel and
cut in half lengthwise. Arrange in greased baking dish. Mix
salt, sugar, and flour. Pour over potatoes. Dot with butter.
Add marshmallows and nuts. Pour cream over all. Bake at
350° about 45 min.

DICED BEETS

Use desired amount of cooked beets. Dice. Cut 2 slices of
bacon into small pieces. Brown until crisp. Add beets and 2
tb. water. Cover until thoroughly heated.

ONIONS

8 soda crackers	2 tb. butter
3 tb. cream	8 eggs
3 Spanish onions	Grated cheese
(or desired amount)	Salt & pepper to taste

Place crackers to cover bottom of flat serving dish. Add cream,
and sliced onions fried golden brown in butter (seasoned with
salt). Break eggs on top of onions. Add salt and pepper.
Sprinkle cheese on whites. Bake at 350° until whites are set.

Holiday Traditions

Through the years several dishes have become traditional at our house. The main meal varies, but these are special "extras."

CHRISTMAS

We join a friend's family one evening before Christmas and make several "go's" of Hard Candy. It's fun for each family member-- making, eating and vieing for originality in combination of flavors and colors. (A mixture of various colors in a clear glass dish or jar makes an attractive gift.)

Pan Dulce, served with cider, is traditional in Argentina. We make it besides an assortment of Christmas cookies. Russian Tea is a refreshing contrast to the sweet sweets.

HARD CANDY

3½ c. sugar
1 c. light syrup
2 c. water

½ t. red coloring
1/8 t. cinnamon oil

Combine sugar, syrup and water. Cook to 300°. Pour on cold, buttered marble slab. Add color and flavor. Use wide spatula or pancake turner (buttered) and quickly work the candy, lifting up outer edge toward center. While still hot, but cool enough to handle slightly, immediately form candy into strips. Quickly cut with scissors or knife--cool. (Use 2 qt. pan. Don't scrape pan.)

Variations: green color--spearmint flavor (or peppermint)
            yellow color--lemon
            black (use 1 t. charcoal)--liquorish (anise)
            Create your own combination of flavors and
              colors.
Butterscotch: Add 1/8 lb. butter
            1 t. salt
            Add butter at 260°.

PRETTY HOLIDAY DIVINITY

3 c. sugar
¾ c. light syrup
¾ c. hot water
¼ t. salt

2 egg whites
1 pkg. red or green gelatin
1 c. chopped nuts
½ c. flaked coconut

Butter sides of heavy 2-qt. saucepan and in it combine first 4
ingredients. Cook, stirring constantly until sugar dissolves
and mixture comes to a boil. Cook to hard ball stage (250°)
without stirring. Remove from heat. Beat egg whites until
soft peaks form; gradually beat in gelatin till stiff peaks form.
Pour hot syrup slowly over egg-white mixture, beating constantly
on mixer at high speed until soft peaks form and mixture starts
to lose its gloss. Stir in nuts and coconut. Drop by teaspoonfuls on waxed paper.

PAN DULCE (Sweet Bread)

2 c. milk
½ c. butter
½ c. sugar
1½ t. salt
1 pkg. dry yeast, or 1
   cake compressed yeast
½ c. warm water

4 eggs (beaten)
Grated rind of 1 orange
1 c. raisins
½ c. nuts, coarsely chopped
1 c. candied fruit
9 c. flour

Scald milk. Pour into large bowl or kettle. Add shortening,
sugar and salt. Dissolve yeast in warm water. When milk has
cooled to lukewarm temperature add yeast and eggs. Beat well.
Add orange rind and 6 c. flour. Beat. Mix remainder of flour
with fruit and nuts. Add to mixture. Knead. (Just enough flour
so dough can be handled.) Cover. Let stand in warm place until double in size. Make into 4 round loaves. Bake 350° for 15
min. Reduce to 325° for 30 minutes. Remove from pan. Brush
with melted butter.

"A merry heart does good like medicine." Prov. 17:22a

SUGAR COOKIES

1 c. shortening (half butter)	1½ t. baking powder
2 c. sugar	1 t. soda
2 eggs	¼ c. milk
5 c. flour (approx.)	1 t. vanilla
1 t. salt	

Cream sugar and shortening. Add flavoring. Add eggs and beat until fluffy. Add sifted dry ingredients alternately with milk. Stir well. Chill in refrigerator several hours. Roll out to 1/4" thickness and cut in fancy shapes. Decorate with colored sugar. Bake at 400°, 8-10 min. If you prefer, decorate with colored icing after they are baked.

RUSSIAN TEA

2 c. sugar	1 c. orange juice
2 c. water	½ c. lemon juice
4 cinnamon sticks	1 c. pineapple juice
1 t. grated lemon rind	12 c. boiling water
3 t. grated orange rind	12 tea bags or 12 t. (heaping) loose tea

Combine sugar and water (2 c.), cinnamon, lemon and orange rind in saucepan. Boil 5 minutes. Remove cinnamon sticks. Add orange, lemon, and pineapple juice. Keep hot. Pour boiling water over tea. Steep 5 min. Combine tea and fruit mixture and serve hot. Serves 12.

NOTE: Entire rind of 1 lemon and of 2 oranges may be boiled with mixture in place of grated rind. Remove with cinnamon sticks.

ORNAMENTS

Crack English walnuts in half. Remove meat. Glue shells together with a string loop at top. Spray with gold or silver paint and hang on tree. These will last many years.

THANKSGIVING

CRANBERRY SAUCE

4 c. fresh cranberries
2 c. sugar
1-2 c. water

Combine cranberries, sugar and water in saucepan. Heat to boiling point, stirring until sugar dissolves. Boil rapidly until berries pop open (about 5 min.).

UNCOOKED PLUM PUDDING

1 pkg. orange gelatin
2 c. boiling water
¾ c. sugar
1 c. raisins
1 c. chopped dates
¾ c. currants

1¼ c. nutmeats
1 t. cinnamon
¼ t. cloves

Mix sugar and gelatin. Add boiling water. Cool. Cook raisins in very little water until soft. Cool. Add fruit, nuts and spices to gelatin. Pour into large ring mold. Serve with whipped cream or vanilla ice cream.

"Whether you eat or drink, do all to the glory of God."
I Cor. 10:31

Miscellaneous

EQUIVALENT MEASUREMENTS

3 teaspoons = 1 tablespoon
4 tablespoons = ¼ cup
16 tablespoons = 1 cup
2 cups = 1 pint

2 pints = 1 quart
4 quarts = 1 gallon
16 ounces = 1 pound

FOOD EQUIVALENTS

1 pound butter = 2 cups
1 pound corn meal = 3 cups
1 pound flour (all purpose) = 4 cups

1 pound raisins = 3 cups
1 pound rice = 2 cups
1 pound sugar = 2 cups

SUBSTITUTIONS

1 ounce chocolate	— —	3 tablespoons cocoa
1 cup cake flour	— —	7/8 cup all-purpose flour
1 tablespoon cornstarch for thickening	— —	2 tablespoons flour

TO MAKE:

Cake flour . . . . remove 2 tablespoons flour from 1 cup of flour and add 2 tablespoons cornstarch.

Sour milk . . . . add one tablespoon vinegar to 1 cup milk. Let set for 20 minutes before using.

COUGH SYRUP

Mix equal portions of glycerine, lemon juice, honey and olive oil. Shake well before using.

Dosage: 1 teaspoon for children, 1 tablespoon for adults as often as needed. This is an effective cough syrup you don't need to be afraid of.

GRANULATED SOAP

1 can lye
3 qts. cold water
¾ c. Borax
4½ lbs. melted fat

Dissolve lye in cold water (use wooden spoon). Add Borax, when dissolved slowly add melted fat. Stir slowly and constantly for 10-15 minutes. Then stir occasionally for the next 24 hours.

PINEAPPLE TIMBAL

1 c. sugar
½ c. butter
Juice enough to moisten
½ loaf fresh bread
   (crustless)
½ c. pineapple

Cream sugar and shortening, add pineapple and crumbled bread. Bake in slow oven 2 hours. Serve warm in place of vegetable or cold with a sauce.

"Godliness with contentment is great gain." I Tim. 6:6

Hints

Eat a good breakfast. You'll eat less the rest of the day ... and feel better!

Buy day old baked foods and store in freezer. Can be frozen for 2-3 months.

Use frozen pork within a few weeks. Pork loses its taste if kept in freezer longer than a month.

Leave an inch of stem on beets before cooking to retain color. They peel easily if dipped in cold water after cooked.

Cut onion at top end instead of root end to prevent them from burning your eyes.

Pour some warm water into empty catsup bottle. Shake well. Use when baking beans.

Wash celery leaves. Drain. Place in plastic bag and put in vegetable pan in refrigerator. Use as seasoning in soups and fillings.

Dry green parsley leaves until crisp. Store in airtight containers and use as seasoning in soups and meat dishes.

Thoroughly dry green mint tea leaves. Store in airtight container. Boil 10 minutes in water and serve as hot drink in water.

Pour a teakettle of boiling water down the kitchen sink drain several times weekly to keep it from clogging.

When cleaning the sink, dish pans or garbage pail with Cleanser, don't rinse until the next dish washing time. Also leave dish cloth unrinsed. Do this several times weekly and you'll have white, unstained sink and containers.

Remove dents from pots and pans by placing dented surface against a firm level object with bumpy surface toward you. Use medium-heavy hammer and tap bump with quick light taps.

Immediately pluck dried leaves and blooms from your house plants. Keeps them clean and gives nicer plants.

Place plants in bath tub, sprinkle with soap suds. Rinse and let set until water drains off. Make this a bi-weekly job and you you'll have healthier, prettier plants.

Put crushed egg shells in glass jar. Cover with hot water. Cover with lid. Let set for several days. Water plants with this water once a week instead of using plant food.

Occasionally water ferns with water from tea grounds.

Cut tops off pretty plastic detergent lotion, etc., containers. Use them to pot house plants.

Air the house daily in winter time. Open doors or windows for 10 minutes upon rising in the morning or just before retiring at night, or during the day when children nap.

If job keeps you indoors, daily step outside or put head out of doors and inhale 10 deep breaths of fresh air. This allows a complete oxygen change in the lungs.

When over-exposed to hot sun rays, dip face (head) in cold water, or swish cold water on face, temples and neck to avoid sinus infection.

Apply vinegar generously to first signs of oak or ivy poisoning. Repeat frequently.

Apply a baking soda pack immediately to bee sting. Use just enough water to moisten soda.

Add 2 tbs. vinegar to 1 gal. lukewarm water when washing windows and see them sparkle!

To remove chewing gum from unwanted places, rub with ice cube. Pick off hard pieces.

Put nails or hooks in the closet low enough for the young child to reach. He then can hang up his own clothes.

HEART TO HEART

Heart to Heart is a broadcast for home-makers that brings a practical Christian approach to marriage, child-training and family living.

In her informal "heart to heart" manner Ella May Miller, mother of three sons and one daughter, comes to grips with those daily perplexing problems every homemaker faces.

Heart to Heart, produced both as a weekly 15-minute broadcast and a daily 5-minute program, is currently released across the nation, in Canada and in the West Indies.

For a schedule of broadcasts or further information about this unique radio broadcast, just write to address below.

Additional copies of this cookbook—50¢ each.

HEART TO HEART®
HARRISONBURG, VIRGINIA